Allyson
We must open
our strength to help
each other grow
to yourself
Blessings

Be good
girl

Be Happy

LOVE
GONE
WRONG

LOVE
GONE
WRONG

by Toni J. Turner

FRIEND PUBLISHING
CHICAGO

I

Cover Designed by: Toni J. Turner
Edited by : Nancy A. Gustafson

Published in the United States of America
Toni J. Turner
Love Gone Wrong
ISBN 0-9643316-4-0
Manufactured in the United States of America
Printed by The Merten Company

Dedication

This book is dedicated to my grandmother, Sue Ella Turner, and my dearest of friends who have moved on to a better life.

John Melvin .... so much joy we shared
Lavoid Perry .... we laughed and danced the nights away
Dawn Turner .... my godchild, our precious Angel... so young
Vermell Beall .... you were always there for me
Marion Brown...... my mother, the secrets you kept
Anthony Turner.... my nephew, I love you
Greg Brown .... My wonderful friend, We will rollerskate again
Allen H. Turner .... My father, no greater place he could be

I will carry all of you in my heart, everyday, for the rest of my life.

Contents

Men Now

Let's Not Trip

Order Form

LOVE GONE WRONG

From My Heart

The best love
from my Heart
is to myself

The best heartbeat
from my Heart is the joy of
my own accomplishments

The warmest Heart
I've ever felt
The most honest Heart
I've ever met

is that of
my own Heart

I Miss

I miss

what's real
what I can hold on to
what's there for me
what makes me feel good
giving all of me
head to toe
seeing you happy
so satisfied
waking up with you
beside me
tasting you in my mouth

I miss

feeling your breath on my ear
early in the morning
throughout the nights
your touch... touching me
so gentle... so loving
strong arms wrapped around me
face between my breasts
sweet words from your
inner soul

I miss

receiving all you have to give

the reality of it all

I miss
what's REAL

Club Lights

Was it the Club Lights
that made you look so fine ?
Was it all that Champagne I drank
to make your lips taste like
a sweet, sweet wine ?

Did my high make you look
so good to me ?
My eyes overlooked the devil
you were to be

All you saw were
your wants and your needs
You never really saw me

I gave you a degree in
Let Me Help You
You showed me your selfishness
You called it
Me baby Me

The Club Lights disappeared
The Champagne wore off
My eyes opened to the taste of a
bitter wine
All that fineness I thought I saw
was nothing but ugliness in the raw

I'm smiling everyday

That devil is off my back
How stupid of me
to let that fool
get me so off track

I Was Missing Me

You ask me if I miss you ?

How could I miss you ?
You tore down
 my dreams
You disappointed
 my hopes
You threw darts at
 my heart
You lied to
 my intelligence
You smudged
 my smile

Now you want to know why
I still have that sparkle in
my eyes
My sparkle is not for
hopes of your return

I let you do these cold
things to me
because...

When I met you
I was missing Me

No Commitment

Let me use you
for my convenience
Call you when I want to

Let me make love to you
when I feel like it
Tell you we are just
sex partners

You meet someone else
and don't call

I don't want to
I don't have to
I don't miss you
I don't feel like it

A cold voice
asks the question
Why are you getting on My Nerves ?

This cold voice
reminds you
I made
No Commitment to you

I Wanted You

I wanted you to be
the right one for me
You were too immature
to make the sacrifice
You did not know how
to make it work

I wanted you to care
You were too carefree

I wanted you to love me
You were too afraid
to be lovable

I wanted you to be there
when I needed you
You were too needy
too busy taking from me

Now you say
you want me back

I'm too scarred

What You Do That For ?

What you do that for ?
Push me off your knee
There was no where to sit

Embarrass me in front of
my friends
What's wrong
Do you like yourself ?

Why don't you like me ?

Why Should I Care ?

Do I care ?
How could I care ?
Your lovemaking is selfish
Your heart sometimes
turns to stone
You act cold as ice
All I see is your back
after we make love
Why should I stay
to care ?

Never Real

I thought
I was afraid to lose you
I never had you
I could not hold on to you
you were never real
Never real to me
Never real to yourself
How can one be afraid to lose
what one never had ?

He Loved Me

It's not easy to get up
He knocked you down
He must be so scarred
to hit you so hard

The arrow aimed
at your heart
Glowing
he lets go of the bow
He loves it
but to show it ?
Such a cold blow

Just think
he said
he loved me

Victim

He took

Kindness for Weakness
Smiles for Innocence
Laughter for Loneliness
Hugs for Hunger
Sex for Stupidity

He could not take... my heart
He could not take... my strength

Now
He compares me to his
next Victim

No innocence in her smile
Coldness is in her laughter
No hugs like before
To her... sex is... just sex

What a challenge he thinks
Little he knows it's
his turn to be

The next Victim

Dream

I miss you like
I miss a sweet dream
because I wanted it
to be that way
Sometimes I felt
you felt the same way
or was I fooling myself ?

How Easy To Forget You

I could never forget you
I'd always miss you
I'd always care

I wanted to remember
everything about us
I wanted you to always
be there

It took one week to
forget you
One week to omit you
One week not to care

You were boring and
stuck on yourself
You were so unaware
Your cold heart stopped
my warm heart
from remembering
you were ever there

I pity you
You'll never know
how to share
your cold heart with
my warm heart and
I'll never be there for you

Rape

I was raped
I tried to escape
The thought still in my mind
Young and naive
it's hard to believe
one would take advantage of youth

Someone shot off part of his face
He looks a disgrace
to the human race

They made no mistake

He now lives in a cell
I hope it's a living hell

I still remember... his smell

So Seldom

People so seldom
say I love you
then it's... too late
or... love goes

I tell you
I Love You
it does not mean
I want you to stay
forever or
I know you'll never go

I just wish you
did not have to go

A Time To Grow

To still feel what's gone
To ungrip the fear... to let go
of what is no longer there

To face reality and walk away
To believe in tomorrow
and to hold on to the future
A time to grow

WOMEN NOW

Women Now

We are strong
We are alone
We are hard workers
sincere, unappreciated

We are the women
males are afraid of

Why is it so hard for a man
to love a strong woman ?

Why are they so afraid ?

Why do they live in the past
tripping on old relationships ?

They say it's a man's world
but we are rising to the top

We were the dreamers
We were the wishers
We were the wannabes in love

Men have so many excuses
We have one question-

Where are all the Good Men ?

The Wall (Where Are The Husbands ?)

I often said
Let's get dressed up
put on our high heel shoes
take a Ghetto Box
and go to The Wall

The Husbands
who will never be...

The Old Mans War
That Greedy War
Killed those that could
and would have been

Our Husbands
Left us
Strong and Alone

One Ready For Me

Could we make a list
of all the qualities we
want in our next man
to make him
Ready for Me ?

You get what you ask for
but you left something
important out
which he did not have

Add one more item
to the list
Wake up and realize
you fell asleep
in the middle
of your prayers
praying for that
Ready for me Man

Next thing you know
you've stopped praying for him
because the list is too long

Try this
just be healthy
honest and loving to me

Crazy

A warm man out there
to satisfy hunger in me
Walk, talk, eat, drink
make wild love to me

Make it mad
Make it crazy
Make it all right with me

I'm a creature of habit
I would say
Wild love drives me CRAZY

Nurture me
feed me
read me baby
Make it all right with me

Explode in me baby
Heaven is where I want
our feelings to be

Surprise

Surprises as a child always brought
happiness, presents, hugs, kisses, smiles
and lots of love

Surprises for a woman today

he did not call
he did not show
he forgot your Birthday
he forgot Valentine's Day
he forgot flowers on Sweetest Day
he did not celebrate Christmas Day

Surprise
he forgot to pick you up New Year's Eve
Surprise
You replaced him with a part time job

Not Me

I didn't leave you sitting at the dinner table
Not Me

I didn't call you a low down Dirty Dog
Not Me

I didn't put sugar in your tank
Not Me

I didn't call the fire department on you and her
Not Me

Did I tear up your clothes ?
Not Me

Did I change my number ?
Not Me

Did I forget your name ?
Now... that... was Me

Peace Of Mind

Busy Busy Busy Busy Busy
Never time to sit down
turn the TV on
eat ice cream
and get fat

I'd rather
play those CDs and
listen to love songs
Smell fresh flowers
throughout my house
Bathe in soothing bubbles
Drink champagne in crystal
Take time to imagine
what he will look like
how wonderful he will be
to feel relaxed
peaceful and childlike

I pity the ones so
unhappily married
no serenity
nor peace of mind
without a man themselves

They are alone
and lonely

Drive

The price to get here
He did not understand
my drive
desire... determination
to be better

My strength
His weakness

my strong soul
his lost soul

our distant hearts

Girlfriends

We talk together
go out together
share secrets
laugh
cry
together

Your disappointments
I know
We help each other
stand up
to face another day
together

No wonder Girlfriends
are more than
Just Friends

My Baby

There's a drought
going on out here
A shortage of true men
By the time men turn
around to go to the well
the world will be a living hell

My clock was ticking and men
were playing games and tricking
women everywhere
I did not have time for that
I wanted to have a baby

Society is cruel when it
comes to this matter
I'm just as good alone, if
not better, than any two that
start out together and end up apart

There'll never be a divorce in our house
There'll never be unhappiness in our house
Because I wanted you

I will punish you when you're wrong
I will hold you when you're hurt
I will be your best friend
You will be my heart
My arms will welcome you
Because I wanted you

He Wants To Marry Me

I'm dying
and he wants to marry me

I've dated him for
more than twenty years
of my life and now
he wants to marry me

My head is bald
Decay... inside my walls
Pain... no longer in my heart
but in my brain
Every part of me I strain
draining my will to
walk again
So weak
no longer can I speak
Morphine has me insane
but he can gain
He wants to marry me

What the hell for ?
So I can die a Mrs.
or for him to try to get a
good night's sleep for the
rest of His life ?

Damn You

Damn you for giving my girlfriend Aids
for being such a cheat
a liar-whore
just a piece of meat

You had no personality, charm, or respect
no sympathy, no regrets

Damn you for all the pain you put her through
Damn you for all the hurt we are going through

Damn you for the rest of your life
Why... did she have to be... your Wife ?

Nephew

I realized one thing from my nephew's death
We are not put on this earth to judge each other
I was disappointed that he never completed high
school
I disapproved of his lifestyle
It was his life not mine to judge

Do we love someone because he's a basketball
player
or because he's a good person ?
He loved his children and was there for them

Some of the most educated have
no time for their children
Should a person be judged by his education,
money or success, the accomplishments
we can brag about ?

He was so proud of me
He loved me so much
I never told him, I love you

He's dead
He died so young
You learn from death

Smile

Good to be alive
Good to be healthy

Nothing like a friend
my forever friends

When life takes a friend
you don't feel alive
you don't feel healthy

Heartaches and memories
where do you store them ?
The heart is strong
You will move on
and smile once more
a bigger smile than before
because
your friends begin
to live through you

Grannie, I'm Missing You

I'm missing your wisdom
big hugs, bright eyes
your warm smiles
you looking at me
seeing yourself in my eyes

My mistakes
My hard head
My way
She would say,
" Why is youth wasted on the young ?"

One day you see a
change in me
Your wisdom and ways
become my way
My eyes like your eyes
You smile and say
It was worth it
I'll forever feel that big hug
envision your warm smile

I'll always miss you

I Lie Alone And Cry

Tonight
I lie alone and cry
I've lost another friend

Heavy tears flood the surface
of my body and open the gates
once more to the pain of
losing another friend

The corners of my eyes sting
from wiping away the tears
that won't stop flowing
I cannot see
My eyes are clouds of blur
My neck and breasts are
soaked in tears
My heart pounds in my head
making it hard for me to breathe
Pain fills my naked body as I
lie in the fetal position
I know so well

Weeping quietly... feeling the
loss of my forever friend
Not to be there by his side
to just hold his hand

I do not scream " Why Lord ?"
Why is not for me to ask

When my best friends died
and my grandmother died
and my mother died
I lay alone and cried

Had the husband in my life
known better,
would he have been better ?
It's not worth the thought

I still lie alone and cry
over the loss of my loved ones
but I don't expect a man to
be there to comfort me
I've found comfort from within
I'm not hurt or disappointed
over another person's lack
of affection or understanding

God has pulled me through
God has helped me find a place to
store all the sadness my heart has
had to endure from death
But, right now, tonight
I will cry myself to sleep
remembering the good times we
shared together
All the times we skated together
as children
Just months ago we skated together
as adults
We've had long conversations

and happy laughter over the years
He kept in touch wherever I
lived, city to city
He was a wonderful friend of
thirty years

Tomorrow I must wake up strong
for all my forever friends
I must continue on my journey to
fulfill my purpose in this life
but tonight
I lie naked and cry myself to sleep
because I have lost
another friend

Young Girls

Hold on to it
Don't let it go
Don't let him sweet talk you
Don't let him know

How little he knows about you
How little he really cares

When you become a woman
he won't be the one that's there

It's your precious body
It's your only life

A young girl has to
hold on to it
Remember that
and keep it tight

My Senior Co-Workers

We have an education
no book can teach
no professor can preach

The road we have walked to get here

Seniority and wisdom go
hand and hand

We are incredible

MEN NOW

The Perfect Man

The perfect man
Is there such a thing ?
You tell me

ten words or less
twenty words or less
thirty words or less

and let's tell the world

Mr. Wonderful

Men scream the question
What do you want from me ?

You reply
TO BE WONDERFUL

They say
WHAT'S THAT ?

One can only smile
to keep from crying

No More Hellos

Are you married ?
Do you have a boyfriend ?
Do you have children ?
Do you live at home ?
Do you live alone ?
Do you have a job ?

Are you bisexual ?
Do you use protection ?
Have you been tested for Aids ?

Do you owe Uncle Sam ?
Do you pay child support ?

Do you have good credit ?
Own any property ?
Are you in debt ?

Fill out this application and
return to the club next week

Whatever happened to
Hello
My name is
What's yours ?
Nice to meet you

Baby He Was Sweet

He look so sweet
he rotten my teeth
Sweet enough to eat

Like candy
sticky and licky
yummy to my tummy

What a sweet piece of meat

Here Comes Slick

He's so slick
He knows every trick
to get money and presents
out of you

He's so cool
He has every tool
to use to get you

What a toilet he is
A turd floating on water

What a joke he is
He thinks he's so smooth

He's just a wipe
He's just a fool

A Dog For A Husband

You think you have a
 good husband
Who you foolin... yourself ?
You know he's no good

You've been married
how long ?
He tried to call me after
one month

How many babies has he
made in the street ?

Hope you have a good
insurance policy on him
because
you have a Dog for a husband

Ex

I met this guy
I married him
We got along just fine
One day I saw a young girl
walking a baby boy that
should have been mine
I stared at the child
I could not believe my eyes
This little twin I see
He was my husband's baby boy
This happened before me
He never mentioned
the child before
I felt betrayed you see
I could never stay married to a man
who did not take care of
his responsibilities

I'm divorced now; he gave me hell
for all the guilt he felt
I'm a much stronger woman
because
I am so Real

Less Than Men

Where are they ?
Laying up somewhere
making more sons ?

Do they know their sons
who carry their invisible
fathers' names ?

Lost angry sons
on the news at night
Like dogs with rabies
ready to bite
mad at the world
looking for a fight
No respect for the
young or elderly
killing anyone in sight
How deep is young anger ?
Less than a man has no Guilt

You have created this
horror we see on the news
poor neighborhoods are
suffering the blues

The Devil has become their father
you were never there to care
The Devil will become the Son
What is to be done ?

It's time for the World to find
these invisible fathers
these less than men
and make them Responsible
for the future that's so out of hand

Hazel Higgens and Ho

Hazel Higgens and Ho
don't live here no mo
I paid $880 dollars to get rid of your a__

Don't call me to cook no pork chops
Don't call me to cut your hair
cause Hazel Higgens and Ho
don't live here no mo

no more cookin
pickin up your mess
no more sex
not at this address

I packed Hazel Higgens and Ho
with your clothes and
federal expressed them to you
out there somewhere

He's Broken

Did you ever keep something
in your life that was broken ?

You threw it away

If he's broken and you
can't fix him
I suggest you throw
him away

Brothers Off Track

Yeah, it's easy My Brother
to get off track
When Grey is buying gifts
and Grey is offering trips
and Old Ms. Grey
is willin to trick... My Brother

Sure she says yes
to any and everything
Her goal is to Control
Total Control

It seems so easy to go with Grey
Born with a silver spoon
in her mouth
and bored to death

I'll buy you Brother
I'll control you Brother
I'll be so sweet
you won't know what hit you
until I've bitten you

I own you... My Brother

Try taking her to church to
see what the Reverend will say
Guess who's coming to dinner
let's see what Momma's gonna say

You can sugar coat it all you want
Grey is still Grey... My Brother

You're Not That Tuff

Blonde hair
blue eyed devil
throw that hair
in my brother's face
you can't handle his pace

Looking for a jock
to lock you up
Never would you look his way
if not for the game
he plays today

Take his money
want his fame
you're not that tuff
to play his game
You can't hang

You can't hide
after an easy ride
what the future holds
in store for you
Play, take, walk away...
Not today

Blow his mind
you're not his kind
He'll blow you away

Strayed

Could it be worse ?
You may be cursed
Try not walking away

If he were gay
what would you say ?
It doesn't matter
he strayed

All your feelings are
on the line
He may have Aids

All your dreams
hopes and wishes
you may be kissing
good-bye today

Here He Comes

Here he comes after
years of being apart
Me mending my broken heart
Here He Comes

After years of living alone
His mistakes have passed me by
Luggage is gone
Here He Comes

Think About It

There's nothing else you
can give me
but to be
a part of me

My World

This is what my eyes have seen
My ears have heard
My heart has felt
What's in my soul

LET'S NOT TRIP

Trippin

They start off telling you
you got it goin' on
and you're great

Here it comes
You're too flashy
Tone down your dress
You live above your means

Tell them a thing or two

Why don't they have
anything to show for living
except jealousy and resentment ?

Be responsible
Stop trippin

GROW UP

Back Stabbers

Smile in your face
Stab you in your back
Insecure, devious, devilish snitches
Heartless, vicious, cold blooded witches
Lying little _____
Working two personalities
Wasting your time and energy
digging yourselves deeper into ditches

For The PMS

A new excuse to give you
a reason to be depressed
and say it's OK

To waste a week
out of every month
to hold yourself back

I don't PMS
I like myself all the time
I have no time for

What was it called
P what ?

So Cold (Users)

One can be
So Cold
Your survival
the only important thing

Victims picked... so carefully
Tactics... so perfect
You were good... so natural
It's life to you
How could you be
So Cold ?

So Cold
leaving behind your victims
as though elephants have
stampeded their hearts

What a wonderful feeling
swinging from one vine
to the next

How could you fall ?
You'd never get caught
You can be
So Cold

So Cold
no joy in your heart
So Cold

your frozen heart
So Cold

So Cold

Don't Lose Yourself

She became so hard
so bitter... so mean
Life with him made her
so bitter... so mean

After spending time with her
I knew I could never stay
to only end up
bitter and mean

Never let a man
make you so hard
Never let
Weakness for Love
kill your
Passion for Life

Wasted Time

She waited
and waited
and waited
for him to realize
she was the right one
for him
She waited years

He married someone else
Something she thought
he'd never do

Never waste your precious
time waiting on a man

Let's Not Get Fat

Let's get fat
Let's get depressed
about him and eat
everything in sight

Let's get bigger and bigger
until everything is too tight
Later, you will really be
depressed because nothing fits
and you're fat
He and everyone else
will love talking about that

The best revenge is to
not get fat

If It Ain't Right

If it ain't right
leave it alone
If it's not your game
don't play it
If it's not what makes
you feel good
forget it
Cause it ain't right

You And The Wind

You see how I act
and know where I've been
You see how I live
You know how I spend
You know what I like
and how I am
If you don't act right
You'll feel nothing but... my wind

A Sweet Dream

I awakened this morning
missing you
Not feeling you
all over me
The after taste of our love

Hunger was in me
No hugs no kisses
no morning sweetness
from your lips

I wanted you
for the rest of my life

Me beside you... forever

I woke up

Worth It

Settle for less
Less never made me happy

I stood alone
I was not afraid to leave
a miserable marriage
I wanted to breathe

My mind was not lazy
I did not take from him

Pain and sorrow
rolled off my back each time
I never looked back

Ups and downs
I've handled alone
Now... I'm grown

Life has taught me well
I am a scholar of wisdom
A rare Queen one would say

I'm one in a million
I feel it everyday

In Time

Funny how lonely you feel
when it's over
to feel half not whole

You want him back
to go through
what he put you through

Do you ?
You'll meet someone
better for you
in time

No More Nuts

When you meet another Nut
and you feel it in your Gut
and you know he's
all wrong for you
Just walk away
smile and say
there's nothing
I can do for you

I've learned from
my mistakes
I've felt my share of
heartaches
My disappointments
were not few

The tear I cried
how hard I tried to improve
so many of you

Comb your hair
Brush your teeth
Clean your nails
to name just a few

I was running a school
for wayward boys
with too much
growing up to do

Finally I stopped playing
Mother and Fool

I thank All of You

Tomorrow

My heart does not ache
from my past
I move forward with my life
No time to waste on regrets
Everyday a new
Another day to try harder
to be better, to improve
to succeed, to fall in love
What a difference a day makes

Thank You

I thank God for giving me direction when no
companion cared.
When my friends died, God gave me peace and
courage.
When heartless relationships came my way to
conquer me,
God gave me wisdom to walk away... I thank you.

I Thank
   The Good
      The Bad
        and
          The Ugly

Without you... there would be no...
Love Gone Wrong.

order form

Company name: _____

Name: _____

Address: _____

City: _____

State: _____ Zip: _____ - _____

Phone #: (   ) _____-_____ Optional

Sales Tax:

Please add 8.75% for books shipped within Illinois

Shipping:

# of books_____ $13.95 per book

$2.00 shipping first book .75 cent for each additional book

Air Mail: $3.50 per book

Payment: TONI J. TURNER

(   ) check (   ) money order (   ) cashier check

Mail Payment to: FRIEND PUBLISHING
                       60 EAST CHESTNUT 311
                       CHICAGO, IL 60611